Look Before You Leap

The Essential Guide for Understanding Each Other Before Marriage

Betsy Summers

CompCare® Publishers
2415 Annapolis Lane
Minneapolis, MN 55441

©1992 Betsy Summers
All rights reserved.
Published in the United States
by CompCare Publishers,
a division of Comprehensive Care Corporation.

Library of Congress Cataloging-in-Publication Data
Summers, Betsy
        Look before you leap!: the essential guide for understanding each other before marriage/Betsy Summers.
p. cm.
Includes bibliographical references.
ISBN 0-89638-299-0
1. Marriage–Problems, exercises, etc. 2.Communication in marriage–Problems, exercises, etc. I. Title.
HQ734.S9765 1993   92-37517
646.7'8–dc20   CIP

Cover design by John Hamilton

Inquiries, orders, and catalog requests should be addressed to
CompCare Publishers
2415 Annapolis Lane
Minneapolis, Minnesota 55441
Call toll free 800/328-3330
or 612/559-4800

6   5   4   3   2   1
97   96   95   94   93   92

CONTENTS

INTRODUCTION

Oftentimes the dividing line between success and failure is information. Whether we are considering a business decision, an investment opportunity, or a romantic endeavor, if a lack of experience or information prevents us from making an intelligent decision, we may need the help or advice of an expert. We may enlist the counsel of a doctor, an accountant, a lawyer, a real estate agent, or some other type of professional to inform and educate us.

Why, then, when it comes to relationships, are we so eager to throw ourselves into a lifelong commitment before we've gathered all the information we need to succeed? Our emotions! We make decisions that will affect us for the rest of our lives based on feelings of love and attachment alone. Romance is an elusive state that cannot be fully explained or understood, and that is its beauty. We need to allow ourselves the experience of "falling in love," revel in the all-consuming feeling of lust, and enjoy the feeling of wanting to spend most of our time with our beloved. However, this is just the beginning of a relationship. The true substance is found after the romance fades and real life begins.

Few things are as destructive to a healthy relationship as lack of communication. To feel close, two people must keep the lines of communication open. Good heart-to-heart communication can help to establish a bond with another human being or strengthen an existing one.

Communication is a learned response. If we don't learn healthy communication skills as children, chances are we will be poorly equipped as adults to communicate effectively. But the art of communication can be learned. We begin by recognizing our fear of revealing ourselves. Somewhere along the way, we may have learned that it is easier and

1

less painful to clam up than to try to get our feelings acknowledged and our needs met. But shutting down does not promote healthy relationships. People need people. People need to know how to talk to one another. We cannot have a healthy relationship without good communication.

The purpose of this book is to teach and encourage couples to communicate. Active communicating gives us the opportunity to learn much about ourselves and others. We may then begin to recognize what our needs are, what qualities are important to us in a partner, and which qualities we are willing to compromise on. We also become aware of potential problem areas within our relationship. With this knowledge, we can make healthier choices for our lives.

Each chapter of this book asks questions about a different issue of concern in many relationships. The answers to the questions express the inner workings of the people responding and provide clues to who the people are.

Some questions in this book address sensitive topics that couples sometimes find difficult to discuss. Because of the discomfort they create, these issues are often overlooked, ignored, or not given the degree of attention they deserve. These topics can be blockades to a healthy relationship, or, if addressed openly and honestly, they can be stepping-stones.

The questions have been constructed to encourage dialogue between couples. A yes or no answer will not suffice. Don't be afraid to expound upon feelings and thoughts, thereby giving useful information to your partner. Learning about each other can be a very rewarding experience for you both.

Be open and honest with yourself and your partner in your answers to these questions. If you discover areas that are troublesome for you or for your relationship, seek help from the sources available to you and try to work through your problems together.

HOW TO USE THIS WORKBOOK

Each chapter is divided into three sections containing questions and activities for you and your partner. Set aside a specific time to work through each section. Some sections will take longer to complete than others. Take your time and don't rush through any of the material.

Complete Sections One and Two alone. Get together with your partner to compare notes after completing each section. Complete Section Three together.

SECTION I. PERSONAL INVENTORY. This section is all about you. It examines the way you perceive yourself, interpret data, and make decisions. It discusses some topics about your family background and reveals what went into the making of you.

SECTION II. POINT OF VIEW. This section covers how you view your partner. What people do tells us more about them than what they say. This section allows you to examine and discuss the impressions your partner has made on you.

SECTION III. COMING TOGETHER. This is where the real fun begins. Work on this section with your partner. You will find out surprising things about each other, learn where compromise is necessary, and get a taste of what married life is all about.

Do not let the format of this workbook limit you. If any of the questions stir your desire for discussion, follow your urge. Most of all, have fun together.

CHAPTER ONE

COMMUNICATION

At one time or another, each of us has been accused of saying something we are positive we never said. Yet our accuser would lay odds on our guilt. We deny; they insist. They accuse; we cringe. We come to know that sinking feeling of being misunderstood. We think maybe we're losing our mind and can't remember what we've told people lately! So we try again: "Well, what I meant was...," only to be hit with," Oh, yeah, well that's not what you said!" We sigh and give up, because we've just been sucked into the black hole of communication.

According to The American Heritage Dictionary, to communicate is to express oneself in such a way as to be readily and clearly understood. However, this is not as simple as it sounds. Several principles of communication need to be understood and practiced before effective communication can take place.

First, men and women speak different languages. Second, they speak for different reasons. Women want conversation; men want information. Women usually ask how and why questions. Men usually ask who, what, where, and when questions.

Third, we communicate in several ways, not just verbally. Body language and inflection and tone of voice are all part of transmitting a message. All components must be in sync if we are to communicate a clear, concise, consistent message. Most researchers agree that daily communication is based more on nonverbal cues than on the actual content of a message.

We need to be aware of how our nonverbal communication affects our partner. We may give a verbal message of approval and permission, but our nonverbal message may be one of disapproval. Naturally, this causes confusion.

A man who tells a woman "I love you" but refuses to make eye contact with her sends a double message. Avoiding eye contact may easily be interpreted as a lack of sincerity. A woman who tells her fiance, "You know I trust you," and then pulls away when he reaches for her also gives a conflicting message. Remember, it's not just what you say; it's also how you say it and what you do that count.

Fourth, never assume anything. Don't assume you automatically know what your partner means. And don't assume he or she understands what you have said. Always ask for clarification. When a couple unites, two distinct languages and cultures come together. We bring our own expectations, experiences, and prejudices to our relationships, and these color everything we say and hear.

What is your definition of early? What is your partner's? If you tell your partner you will drop by early, what does that mean? For you it might mean a few minutes earlier than planned. For him it might mean a few hours earlier. Consider the statement "We will get married soon." A statement like this could mean as soon as next week or as soon as next year. Be specific. Instead of saying early or soon, set a specific time or date. (Just make sure you're both in the same time zone!)

COMMUNICATION TOOLBOX

1. Stick with the issue at hand. Don't bring up situations that happened three months ago (unless that is the topic of discussion).

2. If you are angry, attempt to identify why you feel this way.

3. Pay attention to your own body language.

4. Set aside adequate time to discuss important issues.

5. Don't accuse. Use "I" messages to express feelings. Example: "I feel hurt when you don't call me during the day. It makes me feel as if I'm not a priority in your life" will be received much better than "You never call me anymore. I guess you just don't care about me."

6. Avoid words that exaggerate, like always and never.

Last, develop good listening skills. Listening is an underused skill. Effective communication involves not only giving a message accurately, but having it accurately received as well. One of the greatest gifts you can give your partner is the gift of attentive listening.

LISTENING TOOLBOX

1. Give the speaker your undivided attention.

2. Do not interrupt or put words into the speaker's mouth.

3. Maintain eye contact.

4. When your partner is trying to tell you something, don't tune him or her out by rehearsing what you're going to say next.

5. Repeat or rephrase your partner's statements to prove you're really listening and to make sure you've understood correctly.

6. Pay attention to your partner's nonverbal cues.

7. Acknowledge or validate the speaker's feelings.

8. Do not be concerned with "winning" an argument or discussion. Remember: Either both of you win or neither of you wins.

As you begin this first section, pay special attention to your partner's verbal and nonverbal communication. Be honest in your responses. Don't assume you already know how your partner will respond. Be prepared to learn about each other's style of communication.

SECTION I

Personal Inventory

This section asks questions about what you learned about interacting with others as you were growing up. Answer the questions in this section on your own. When you are done, compare your answers with your partner's.

GROWING UP

Using the scale of 1-5 below, choose the number that most closely represents your response.

  1 — Strongly Agree
  2 — Agree
  3 — Not Sure
  4 — Disagree
  5 — Strongly Disagree

_____ 1. If I had a problem while growing up, I could talk to one or both of my parents about it.

_____ 2. As a child, I was heard and my feelings were validated.

_____ 3. My family discussed things openly; we had no secrets.

_____ 4. In my family we could disagree but still get along.

_____ 5. Yelling and screaming were common forms of communication in my family.

_____ 6. It is acceptable for men to cry.

_____ 7. Manipulation was used often in my family.

_____ 8. My family used the "silent treatment" to express disapproval or anger.

_____ 9. I usually had a clear understanding of what my parents expected of me.

_____ 10. I still communicate with some members of my family.

▲▲▲▲▲▲▲▲▲▲▲▲▲▲▲▲▲▲▲▲▲▲▲▲▲▲▲▲▲▲▲▲▲▲▲▲

DO YOU...?

In response to the following questions, answer Never, Rarely, Sometimes, Often, or Always.

Do you...

1. Use manipulations such as "If you really loved me, you would..."?

2. Interrupt people before they have finished their thought?

3. Accuse, belittle, or call your partner a name when you are feeling frustrated during an argument?

4. Threaten to leave, walk out, or withhold pleasure when things don't go your way?

5. "Clam up" when you don't want to talk?

6. Act out your anger by slamming doors, throwing things, or punching the walls?

7. Become physically or sexually abusive?

8. Admit when you are wrong?

9. Acknowledge what others have said to you; allow them to have their feelings?

10. Try to justify your actions when people disagree with you?

11. Become nervous or uncomfortable when people express disapproval of you or your actions?

12. Tell people right away when they offend you?

13. Sulk, pout, or stew over wrongs done to you?

14. Hesitate to ask for what you want or need?

15. Try to guess what your partner's needs are?

▲▲▲▲▲▲▲▲▲▲▲▲▲▲▲▲▲▲▲▲▲▲▲▲▲▲▲▲▲▲▲

SECTION II

Point of View

This section deals with how you view your partner. Work on this section by yourself, then get together and compare notes.

MY PARTNER IS...

1.   Rate the following statements either "True" or "False."

My partner...

_____ a. Is very attentive when I speak.

_____ b. Expresses feelings and emotions openly.

_____ c. Likes to be the center of attention at gatherings.

_____ d. Almost always remembers what I have said.

_____ e. Is usually willing to hear another's viewpoint even if it differs from his or her own.

_____ f. Likes to debate.

_____ g. Chooses words carefully before speaking.

_____ h. Is easy to talk to about anything.

_____ i. Is quick to criticize.

_____ j. Employs a double standard when talking about people of the opposite sex.

2.   Write the first five words that come to mind that describe your partner's listening skills.

_____

_____

_____

▲▲▲▲▲▲▲▲▲▲▲▲▲▲▲▲▲▲▲▲▲▲▲▲▲▲▲▲▲▲▲▲▲▲

3. How does your partner communicate anger? (Include any non-verbal clues that apply, such as facial expressions, clenched fists, nail biting.)

_____

_____

_____

_____

_____

_____

_____

_____

_____

_____

4. When was the last time your partner cried? What were the circumstances and how did you respond?

_____

_____

_____

_____

_____

_____

_____

_____

_____

_____

5. Because of your hectic schedules, you haven't seen your partner for several weeks. Finally you get together for an intimate dinner at your place. You're talking, laughing, and enjoying each other's company when suddenly the phone rings. You answer it. It's a distraught friend who needs to talk. Forty-five minutes later you rejoin your partner. What happens next?

▲▲▲▲▲▲▲▲▲▲▲▲▲▲▲▲▲▲▲▲▲▲▲▲▲▲▲▲▲▲▲▲▲▲

SECTION III

Coming Together

1. List three of your communication needs that you want your part-
    ner to know about. Explain why each need is important to you.

    _____

    _____

    _____

    _____

    _____

    _____

    _____

    _____

    _____

    _____

2. a. What is your reaction to the following statement:

    Silence is one of the most vicious, destructive communication
    techniques. Silence can communicate dissatisfaction, con
    tempt, anger, or empathy. Many people use silence as a
    weapon.

    _____

    _____

    _____

    _____

    _____

    _____

    _____

b. How do you feel when someone you love gives you the "silent treatment"?

_____

_____

_____

_____

_____

_____

_____

_____

_____

_____

3. Your partner surprises you by sporting a new haircut. You think it looks awful. How do you respond when your partner asks, "Well, what do you think"?

_____

_____

_____

_____

_____

_____

_____

_____

_____

4.   What is your opinion about resolving conflicts before going to sleep at night?

5.   You and your partner don't see eye to eye on a major issue, such as money, sex, children, career, or in-laws. How do you resolve the conflict?

CHAPTER TWO

MORALS AND PRINCIPLES

Our morals and principles form the foundation of who we are. They are our personal system of right and wrong. They are deeply ingrained in us and are important expressions of our character.

We acquire our morals and principles from various influences. They can be passed down from generation to generation, as a part of our family framework, formed on our own, and assimilated through social mores.

Our morals and principles govern our lives. They direct how we will handle life situations. We usually don't give much thought to our morals and principles until a situation demands it. When we are called to make a decision, voice our opinion, or assess circumstances, then we become aware of the need to define our morals and principles. In other words, we take a stand.

If our morals and principles differ greatly from our partner's, there will be differences in the way we view the world and how we live our lives. This is important to remember when choosing a partner. Our morals and principles define who we are. They are not easily changed. Attempts to project our personal system of right and wrong on our partner will usually lead to frustration and disappointment.

▲▲▲▲▲▲▲▲▲▲▲▲▲▲▲▲▲▲▲▲▲▲▲▲▲▲▲▲▲▲▲▲▲▲▲▲

This doesn't mean we can not influence our partner or our partner can not influence us. Change is part of any relationship. There must be give and take. But, hopefully, each person will influence the other for the best. Our input should serve to raise the other's morals and principles not lower them.

▲▲▲▲▲▲▲▲▲▲▲▲▲▲▲▲▲▲▲▲▲▲▲▲▲▲▲▲▲▲▲▲▲▲▲

SECTION I

Personal Inventory

After you complete this section compare notes with your partner.

1. Fill in the blanks:

    a. My family is politically_____.

    b. My family has_____prejudices.

    c. I believe abortion is_____.

    d. Birth control is primarily _____ responsibility.

    e. I believe homosexuals are_____.

    f. I believe it is _____ to seek professional counseling.

    g. Religion is_____.

    h. A "woman's place" is_____.

    i. Premarital sex between consenting adults is_____.

    j. Capital punishment is _____.

2. Circle the number that most closely represents where you fit on the scale below.

Faithful	1 2 3 4 5	Unfaithful
Honest	1 2 3 4 5	Dishonest
Flexible	1 2 3 4 5	Inflexible
Leader	1 2 3 4 5	Follower
Open-minded	1 2 3 4 5	Closed-minded
Outgoing	1 2 3 4 5	Shy
Courageous	1 2 3 4 5	Cowardly
Conservative	1 2 3 4 5	Liberal
Competitive	1 2 3 4 5	Noncompetitive
Rigid	1 2 3 4 5	Relaxed
Funny	1 2 3 4 5	Somber
Independent	1 2 3 4 5	Dependent
Thoughtful	1 2 3 4 5	Thoughtless

3. Briefly state your beliefs about God or a Higher Being.

_____

_____

_____

_____

_____

_____

_____

_____

▲▲▲▲▲▲▲▲▲▲▲▲▲▲▲▲▲▲▲▲▲▲▲▲▲▲▲▲▲▲▲▲▲▲▲▲

4. You have just won $10,000 in the state lottery. How would you spend the money?

_____

_____

_____

_____

_____

_____

_____

_____

_____

_____

5. What are your thoughts on living together before marriage?

_____

_____

_____

_____

_____

_____

_____

_____

_____

_____

_____

▲▲▲▲▲▲▲▲▲▲▲▲▲▲▲▲▲▲▲▲▲▲▲▲▲▲▲▲▲▲▲▲

SECTION II

Point of View

After you have completed this section compare notes with your partner.

1. Answer the following either True or False.

    My partner...

    ____ a. Shares my political beliefs.

    ____ b. Has never lied to me.

    ____ c. Is almost always on time.

    ____ d. Always fulfills his/her promises.

    ____ e. Obeys the law.

    ____ f. Is very generous.

    ____ g. Gives freely of his/her time.

    ____ h. Is an excellent role model.

    ____ i. Can be trusted with a secret.

    ____ j. Makes me feel good about who I am.

▲▲▲▲▲▲▲▲▲▲▲▲▲▲▲▲▲▲▲▲▲▲▲▲▲▲▲▲▲▲▲▲▲▲

2.   Make a list of the character traits, beginning with the most important, that you find attractive about your partner.

_____

_____

_____

_____

_____

_____

_____

_____

_____

_____

3.   What movie or television character most closely reminds you of your partner? Why?

_____

_____

_____

_____

_____

_____

_____

_____

_____

_____

4. What one character "fault" would you like to change in your partner?

_____

_____

_____

_____

_____

_____

_____

_____

_____

5. Describe a memorable event or time when your partner's best character traits were put to the test.

_____

_____

_____

_____

_____

_____

_____

_____

_____

_____

_____

_____

SECTION III

Coming Together

1. Working together complete the following story. The main characters are...tada...you and your partner (you play yourselves). For each space only ONE response may be submitted. Be yourself. Here we go.

You plan to meet another couple for dinner and a movie of your choice. You and your partner have agreed to eat at_____ , because you have the taste for_____food. The movie is_____. You're ready to go. But she is still in the bathroom doing whatever it is that women do. Finally, she joins you. She looks great; but, now you're twenty minutes late. You say, "_____ ," as you slam the car door and peel out of the driveway.

You can't believe he's doing fifty in a thirty-five mph zone. Great, he just ran a red light, and pulls up to park in the handicap space at the restaurant. Your reaction to his disregard of the speed limit and parking laws is,"_____."

She makes you late <u>and</u> she complains about your driving. Women! Hey, your buddy and his date already have a table. You notice his zipper is open when he stands to greet you. You say, " _____ _____ ," as you take your seat and order a drink.

Well into the meal your partner has already had one drink too many. But he signals the waiter and orders another drink. You lean over and say, "_____."
But there's no talking to him now. You turn your attention to his buddy.

You know how many drinks you can handle. Whoa, she's getting a bit friendly with your buddy. She touches his hand, laughs at his joke, and gazes into his eyes. Your buddy soaks it all in. You, _____

_____ to show your disapproval.

Your guy is obviously uptight and a bit drunk. But when it comes time to leave the restaurant he insists on driving everyone to the theater.

How does the evening end?

_____

_____

_____

_____

_____

_____

_____

_____

_____

_____

_____

_____

_____

_____

_____

_____

_____

2. Consider the following situations. In the spaces provided write:

A—if you agree with the action

B—if you disagree, but are willing to compromise

C—if you strongly disagree. Action goes against your morals and principles.

____ a. Invite a Jehovah's Witness in to talk about salvation.

____ b. Donate money to an established charitable organiza tion.

____ c. Your partner wants to raise your children in a religion other than your own.

____ d. Give money to a homeless person on the street.

____ e. Donate food, old clothes, or other items to food shelves, Goodwill, Salvation Army.

____ f. Cheat at a game.

____ g. Cheat on your income taxes.

____ h. Lie on your resume.

____ i. Lie to your partner if the truth would be detrimental to your relationship.

____ j Take supplies from work.

____ k. Purchase a lottery ticket each week.

____ l. Bet money at the track.

____ m. Buy stolen merchandise.

____ n. Sell illegal drugs

____ o. Repeat racist jokes.

____ p. You scratch a parked car. No one sees you. You leave the scene without a note.

____ q. Rent an X-rated video.

____ r. Correspond with a convicted felon.

▲▲▲▲▲▲▲▲▲▲▲▲▲▲▲▲▲▲▲▲▲▲▲▲▲▲▲▲▲▲▲▲▲▲

3. After shopping at your neighborhood supermarket you find a wallet in the parking lot. The wallet contains approximately $500.00 and no identification. What would you do?

_____

_____

_____

_____

_____

_____

_____

4. You suspect your brother-in-law is physically and sexually abusing his children. How do you deal with this situation?

_____

_____

_____

_____

_____

_____

5. How would you react if your sister told you she was a lesbian?

_____

_____

_____

_____

_____

_____

6. You and your partner are enjoying a quiet evening at home. You decide to play truth or dare. Your partner confesses that before you two met he/she had a long time affair with a married person. How do you respond?

_____

_____

_____

_____

_____

_____

_____

_____

_____

_____

_____

_____

7. List three reasons why you would or would not choose to sign an organ donor card.

_____

_____

_____

_____

_____

CHAPTER THREE

SEX

Sex is one of the most intimate forms of communication and plays a major role in relationships. It is an expression of feeling and fulfills a basic human need. Our need for sex ranges from physical pleasure to emotional release.

Generally speaking, men and women view sex differently and have different sexual needs. But more importantly, individual views and needs vary. Before we can satisfy our partner's sexual needs, we must first learn what those specific needs are. We must be able to have an open dialog about sex both in and out of the bedroom.

Initially, sex may be the focal point of our relationship. But the sexual intensity that is common during the first six to twelve months of a relationship mellows with time. As the relationship matures, the focus shifts from sex to other areas of the relationship. Some of us panic at this point. We feel disillusioned with our partner and we wonder where the fireworks have gone.

Sex does not disappear but tends to find its proper place in the relationship. If we have matured as a couple, then all areas of our relationship will benefit.

In this time of AIDS and other sexually transmitted diseases, it is important to realize that sex has become a life-and-death issue. We must take responsibility for our sexual well-being, for our sake as well as for our partner's.

As you begin this chapter, apply the skills you learned in the chapter on communication. Be specific, honest, and clear about your needs and wants. Listen to your partner. Don't assume you know what all men or all women desire sexually. Be prepared to listen and learn about your partner's very individual sexual needs.

▲▲▲▲▲▲▲▲▲▲▲▲▲▲▲▲▲▲▲▲▲▲▲▲▲▲▲▲▲▲▲▲

SECTION I

Personal Inventory

Today, out of necessity, it is becoming more common to inquire about someone's sexual history before engaging in intimate relations. Complete the following sex history questionnaire. When you have finished, compare notes with your partner.

REMEMBERING

1. As a child, where did you get most of your information about sex? Were you able to discuss sex openly with your parents?

_____

_____

_____

_____

_____

_____

_____

_____

_____

_____

_____

_____

_____

_____

■▲▲▲▲▲▲▲▲▲▲▲▲▲▲▲▲▲▲▲▲▲▲▲▲▲▲▲▲▲▲▲▲▲▲▲

2. How did your parents show their affection for each other?

_____

_____

_____

_____

_____

_____

_____

3. How did your parents display affection toward you?

_____

_____

_____

_____

_____

_____

_____

4. What information about sex did you receive from your church, Sunday school class, or other religious organizations?

_____

_____

_____

_____

_____

_____

5.   How old were you when you first masturbated? How did you feel about doing it?

_____

_____

_____

_____

_____

_____

6.   What were you told about masturbation from parents, sex education teachers, and others?

_____

_____

_____

_____

_____

_____

7.   When did you have your first wet dream? What was your reaction to it?

_____

_____

_____

_____

_____

_____

8. At what age did you begin to menstruate? Who explained menstruation to you? How did you feel about yourself when menstruation began?

9. When you learned about your genitals, were you taught the correct names, or was slang used to describe them?

10. Have you ever thought of sex as something dirty?

▲▲▲▲▲▲▲▲▲▲▲▲▲▲▲▲▲▲▲▲▲▲▲▲▲▲▲▲▲▲▲▲▲▲▲▲

SEXUAL EXPERIENCES

1. How old were you when you started dating?

_____

_____

2. Did you ever feel pressured by your first partner to engage in heavy petting or sex? How did you handle the situation?

_____

_____

_____

_____

_____

_____

_____

3. What type of petting was acceptable to you? Unacceptable?

_____

_____

_____

_____

_____

_____

_____

_____

_____

4.   At what age did you first have intercourse? Briefly describe what it was like, how you felt during the act, where it happened, and how you felt about it afterwards.

_____

_____

_____

_____

_____

_____

_____

_____

_____

_____

_____

_____

_____

_____

5.   How long did you remain involved with your first sexual partner?

_____

_____

6.   What type of contraception did you use, if any?

_____

_____

_____

_____

▲▲

7.   Were you ever raped, sodomized, or sexually assaulted in any way? Have you ever raped, sodomized, or sexually assaulted another person?

8.   Have you ever experimented sexually with someone of the same sex? If not, what do you think it would be like?

9.   What sexually transmitted diseases, if any, have you had? How did you feel about the person who infected you?

10.   How many sexual partners have you had?

SEXUAL ATTITUDES AND BELIEFS

1. What kinds of sexual activities do you prefer? Is there anything that makes you uncomfortable or embarrassed?

2. What are your thoughts on masturbation? How often do you masturbate? How would you feel about masturbating in front of your partner? How do you feel about mutual masturbation?

3. What are your thoughts on oral sex? Anal sex?

_____

_____

_____

_____

_____

_____

_____

_____

_____

_____

4. What types of things would your ideal sexual partner need to know about your needs and desires?

_____

_____

_____

_____

_____

_____

_____

_____

_____

_____

5. Have you ever used a sexual aid such as a vibrator, dildo, or other adult toy? Would you object to trying one? Why or why not?

6. How important is foreplay? Describe briefly what you like and dis-like about foreplay.

7. Where does erotic literature fit into your views on sex?

8. Would you be willing to videotape or have photographs taken of you and your partner's sexual relations? Why or why not?

9. Do you prefer to "talk dirty" or use more clinical terms for sexual acts?

_____

_____

_____

_____

_____

_____

_____

_____

_____

_____

10. What is your overall attitude about sex?

_____

_____

_____

_____

_____

_____

_____

_____

_____

_____

_____

SECTION II

Point of View

1.   Rate the following statements either True or False.

My partner...

_____ a.   Is comfortable talking with me about sexual issues.

_____ b.   Is more sexually experienced than I am.

_____ c.   Is willing to take responsibility for birth control.

_____ d.   Can show affection toward me without it leading to sexual intercourse.

_____ e.   Has a healthy attitude toward sex.

_____ f.   Is comfortable with my physical appearance.

_____ g.   Is sensitive to my sexual needs.

_____ h.   Has always been faithful to me.

_____ i.   Is very romantic.

_____ j.   Has very sexist attitudes.

▲▲▲▲▲▲▲▲▲▲▲▲▲▲▲▲▲▲▲▲▲▲▲▲▲▲▲▲▲▲▲▲▲▲▲▲▲▲▲

2. Give a head-to-toe description of your partner. Highlight the physical features that you find attractive.

▲▲▲▲▲▲▲▲▲▲▲▲▲▲▲▲▲▲▲▲▲▲▲▲▲▲▲▲▲▲▲▲▲▲▲▲

3.   Physical features aside, what other qualities do you find sexy about your partner?

_____

_____

_____

_____

_____

_____

_____

_____

_____

_____

_____

4.   How do you feel about your partner's sexual history? Do you think your partner should be tested for AIDS?

_____

_____

_____

_____

_____

_____

_____

_____

_____

_____

_____

Coming Together

1. Do something enjoyable together. See a movie, go out to dinner, play miniature golf, or do any activity that will help you relax and feel close to your partner. After you return, plan your ideal wedding night. Make sure you have plenty of time and privacy. To help with this activity, dim the lights, put on your favorite music, have some appetizers and seltzer, or do anything else that creates a romantic atmosphere. Even if you have been intimately involved with one another for months, plan your ideal wedding night as if it is your first shared sexual and sensual experience.

   Here are a few questions for you to answer when making your plans:

   Where will you spend your wedding night?

   _____

   _____

   _____

   _____

   _____

   What will you be wearing . . . or not wearing?

   _____

   _____

   _____

   _____

   _____

   _____

What do you want to do sexually?

_____

_____

_____

_____

_____

_____

_____

_____

_____

What sexual fantasy would you like to share with your new spouse?

_____

_____

_____

_____

_____

_____

_____

_____

_____

_____

_____

_____

Be specific, and include as many details as possible. Have fun making plans for the night from beginning to end.

▲▲▲▲▲▲▲▲▲▲▲▲▲▲▲▲▲▲▲▲▲▲▲▲▲▲▲▲▲▲▲▲▲▲▲▲▲▲

2. What type of birth control will you use? Who will be responsible for birth control?

_____

_____

_____

_____

_____

_____

CONTRACEPTIVES TOOLBOX

PILL—97%–99% effective. Side effects: weight gain, nausea, depression. Benefits: decreased blood loss, reduced menstrual cramps, some protection against ovarian and endometrial cancers.

CONDOM—98%–99% effective. Side effects: allergic reaction in some users. Benefits: aids in the prevention of sexually transmitted diseases.

INTRAUTERINE DEVICE (IUD)—95%–98% effective. Side effects: spotting or cramping, heavier periods, increased incidence of pelvic infection.

DIAPHRAGM—97% effective. Side effects: recurrent bladder infections, vaginitis.

FOAM/SUPPOSITORIES—95%–97% effective (if used with another form of birth control). Side effects: allergic reaction in some users.

SPONGE—92%–95% effective. Side effects: allergic reactions in some users.

MALE/FEMALE STERILIZATION—99.6% effective. Side effects: none, except those associated with surgery.

3. If your partner asked you to do something sexual that you found distasteful, what would you do?

_____

_____

_____

_____

_____

_____

4. Which of you talks more freely about his or her sex life and previous romances? How does this make the other partner feel?

_____

_____

_____

_____

_____

_____

_____

_____

_____

_____

On the drawings on the next two pages, use a green pen or pencil to mark the places where you like to be touched. Then use a red pen or pencil to mark the places where you don't like to be touched. Use symbols to indicate touch by hand, mouth, or both.

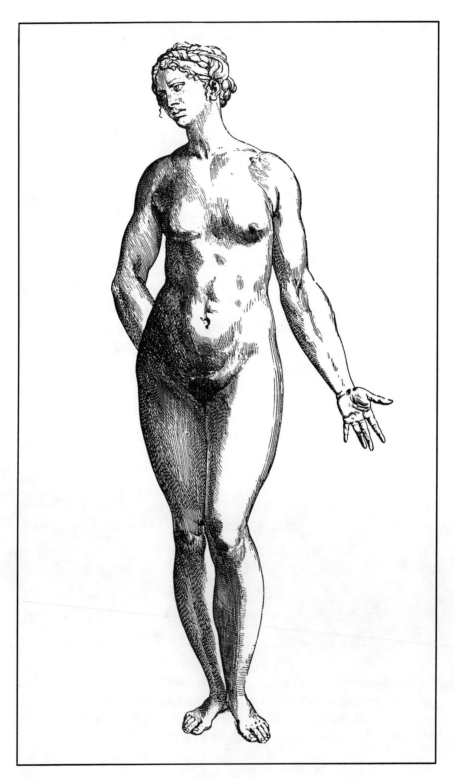

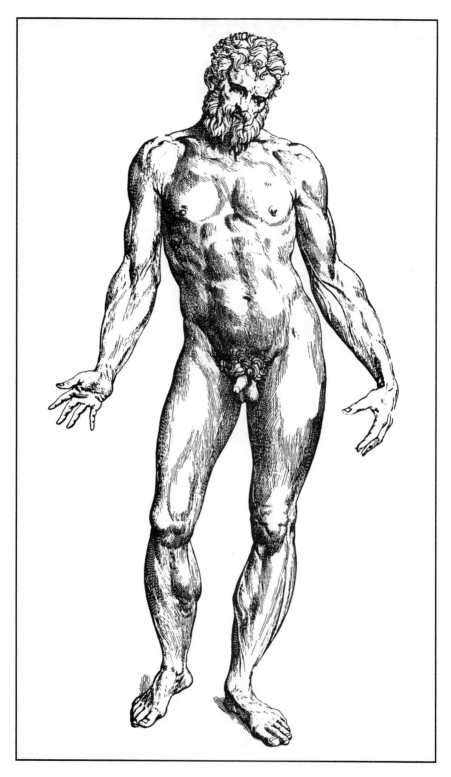

As you fill in the drawing, discuss the following with your partner. Feel free to make notes following each question.

Whose responsibility is it to initiate sex?

_____

_____

_____

_____

_____

_____

_____

_____

_____

How often do you like to have intercourse?

_____

_____

_____

_____

_____

_____

_____

_____

_____

_____

Who is responsible for your orgasm?

How do you feel about asking for what you want from your partner while having sex?

What are your thoughts on multiple orgasms? On faking orgasm?

_____

_____

_____

_____

_____

_____

_____

_____

_____

_____

_____

What type of sexual experimenting would you like to do?

_____

_____

_____

_____

_____

_____

_____

_____

_____

_____

CHAPTER FOUR

PERSONAL HABITS

Who doesn't have some habit, no matter how small, that isn't just a bit irritating? Maybe we pick our teeth, twirl our hair, eat loudly, smoke, or maybe we're just plain sloppy. Maybe we're always late or too organized, our chatter drives people crazy, or worse, our driving has convinced our family and friends that it is possible to get a license through a matchbook cover offer.

How we spend our free time is as much a reflection of our personal habits as our idiosyncrasies. It's not so bad if we collect stamps, but what if we collect bugs? Are we couch potatoes or athletes? Are we competitive or noncompetitive? How we spend our free time says a lot about who we are.

What is so irritating about our partner squeezing the toothpaste tube in the middle, hanging nylons up in the bathroom, or watching twelve straight hours of the sports channel when we love him or her so much? Lots!

Most of what we overlook in the beginning of a relationship becomes annoying once we move into "The Comfort Zone." We all know that shift in a relationship: all of a sudden he's running around the house in his boxer shorts and she colors her hair while he's home! For some reason, when we "let our hair down," we let our opinions out as well.

The best approach is to be realistic. No one is perfect; we all have our idiosyncrasies. No matter how honest we are with each other, things will just sort of "emerge" after a few months or years of matrimony. Relax. It's all part of living together.

SECTION I

Personal Inventory

1. For statements a–o, based on the scale of 1–5 below, choose the number that most closely represents your response.

   1—Always
   2—Quite often
   3—Sometimes
   4—Very seldom
   5—Never

   ____ a.   I am on time for business appointments.

   ____ b.   I am on time for social activities.

   ____ c.   My closet is neat and orderly.

   ____ d.   Profanity is a regular part of my vocabulary.

   ____ e.   I watch five or more hours of television per week.

   ____ f.   I engage in physical activities.

   ____ g.   I go to bed after midnight.

   ____ h.   I read nonfiction books.

   ____ i.   I attend cultural events and activities.

   ____ j.   I drink milk straight from the carton.

   ____ k.   I leave dirty dishes in the sink.

   ____ l.   I meet deadlines.

   ____ m.   I spend time alone.

   ____ n.   I do not let things bother me.

   ____ o.   I complain when things don't go my way.

2.　What are your favorite hobbies?

_____

_____

_____

_____

_____

_____

_____

3.　Which of your hobbies would you like to do with your partner?

_____

_____

_____

_____

_____

_____

4.　What types of pets would you want?

_____

_____

_____

_____

_____

5.   What do you do to relieve stress?

_____

_____

_____

_____

_____

_____

_____

_____

6.   Describe your typical week.

_____

_____

_____

_____

_____

_____

_____

_____

_____

_____

_____

_____

_____

_____

SECTION II

Point of View

1. Rate the following either True or False.

   My partner...

   ____ a. Is punctual.

   ____ b. Has excellent taste in clothes and fashion.

   ____ c. Is neat and organized.

   ____ d. Is adventuresome.

   ____ e. Is spontaneous.

   ____ f. Often makes me laugh.

   ____ g. Loves the "night life," going to clubs and parties, etc.

   ____ h. Likes to spend time alone.

   ____ i. Likes to work more than play.

   ____ j. Is athletic.

   ____ k. Remembers birthdays, anniversaries, and special occasions.

   ____ l. Gives gifts and cards for no special reason.

   ____ m. Is polite and courteous.

   ____ n. Has unhealthy habits.

   ____ o. Has extreme mood swings.

2. When was the last time your partner did something that drove you crazy? What was it that he or she did?

_____

_____

_____

_____

_____

_____

_____

_____

_____

_____

3. What makes you and your partner compatible?

_____

_____

_____

_____

_____

_____

_____

_____

_____

_____

4. What is the one thing you are absolutely certain would make your partner feel happy?

_____

_____

_____

_____

_____

_____

_____

_____

_____

_____

_____

▲▲▲▲▲▲▲▲▲▲▲▲▲▲▲▲▲▲▲▲▲▲▲▲▲▲▲▲▲▲▲▲▲▲

SECTION III

Coming Together

1. Look at the picture on the next page. Do you see anything wrong with this scene? If you find something wrong with it, jot it down.

His List	Her List

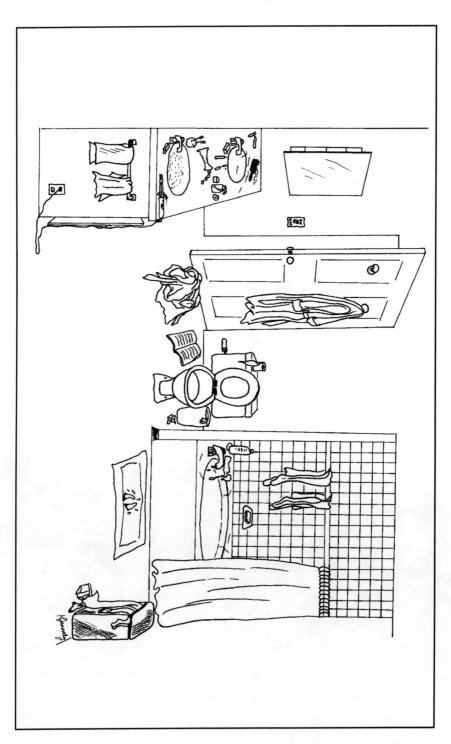

2. Compare your views on the following marriage-busting issues:

   a. toilet seat—up or down?

   _____

   _____

   b. toothpaste—big squeeze or neat roll?

   _____

   _____

   c. morning rituals—radio, talk show, newspaper, or
   conversation?

   _____

   _____

   _____

   _____

   _____

   _____

   d. bedroom windows—open or closed at night?

   _____

   _____

   e. long-distance service—AT&T, Sprint, or MCI?

   _____

   _____

   f. toilet paper—over or under?

   _____

g. ring in the bathtub—cleaned out or left for the next person?

_____

_____

_____

h. surprise guests—welcome or not?

_____

_____

_____

_____

_____

i. punctuality—to call or not to call?

_____

_____

_____

_____

_____

j. kitchen duties—his, hers, or shared?

_____

_____

_____

_____

_____

Television
List a few of your favorites.

	His	**Hers**
Sit Coms	_____	_____
Sports	_____	_____
Drama	_____	_____
Public Television	_____	_____
Game Shows	_____	_____
How To	_____	_____
Soaps	_____	_____
Infomercials	_____	_____
News	_____	_____
Others	_____	_____
Do you want cable?	_____	_____

Music
List your favorite kinds of music and artists

His   **Hers**

_____   _____

_____   _____

_____   _____

_____   _____

_____   _____

_____   _____

_____   _____

_____   _____

_____   _____

_____   _____

_____   _____

_____   _____

What's your favorite radio station?

_____   _____

How much money do you spend on CD's and cassettes?

_____   _____

Do you like to go to concerts?

_____   _____

CHAPTER FIVE

MONEY

According to marriage statistics, money is the number-one subject of disagreement between couples. Surprised? Probably not. We all deal with money issues.

We can't escape the advertisements that scream, Buy me! A certain part of our psyche latches on and responds: Yes, yes, I've got to have it now! We lose all sense of reason and control. We tell ourselves that even though we may not have the cash on hand, we do have plastic power.

Mastercard, VISA, Discover, American Express, countless department-store cards, gas cards, and other buy-now-pay-later devices lure us into debt. Finance charges alone eat up a good percentage of our income. And still we buy.

Money can be a controlling factor in our lives. Some of us are motivated by money; others see money as a necessary evil. Unfortunately, our culture equates success with how much money we have rather than how content we are with our lives. The pursuit of money requires dedication, discipline, and responsibility.

Economic factors may necessitate having a two-income household to make ends meet. In our quest for financial gain, we forfeit much and make many compromises in our daily living. Couples need to evaluate their goals and desires to make sure both partners define success in the same way.

When we get a sense of what money means to our partner and to ourselves, we recognize the realities of our financial status and its limitations. Whether we have a lot or a little, we need to control our money, not let it control us.

SECTION I

Personal Inventory

1. Fill in the blanks:

    a. Growing up,_____controlled the money in our family.

    b. My parents believed credit was a_____thing.

    c. I believe credit is a_____thing.

    d. To me, money means_____.

    e. I'm proud to say that I own my own_____.

    f. I _____balancing my checkbook.

    g. I think financial planners are_____.

    h. Life insurance is_____.

    i. I have _____credit cards.

    j. It is_____for a woman to have a career.

2. Based on the scale below, choose the number that most closely represents your response.

    1—Very Important
    2—Somewhat Important
    3—Not important

    _____ a. Setting financial goals and living on a budget.

    _____ b. Planning for retirement.

    _____ c. Being financially secure.

    _____ d. Owning a house.

    _____ e. Being free of debt.

    _____ f. Having money in savings.

    _____ g. Having a good credit rating.

    _____ h. One parent staying at home full time with young children.

_____ i.   Investing in stocks and bonds.

_____ j.   Saving for your children's college education.

3.   How would you feel if your partner earned more money than you?

_____

_____

_____

_____

_____

_____

_____

4.   What's your opinion of the "what's-mine-is-yours-and-what's yours-is-mine" philosophy?

_____

_____

_____

_____

_____

_____

_____

_____

_____

_____

5. Where does career fall on your list of priorities?

6. What is "woman's work"? "Man's work"?

▲▲▲▲▲▲▲▲▲▲▲▲▲▲▲▲▲▲▲▲▲▲▲▲▲▲▲▲▲▲▲▲▲▲

SECTION II

Point of View

1. Answer the following either True or False.

   My partner...

   _____ a.   Spends money wisely.

   _____ b.   Spends too much money on hobbies and "toys."

   _____ c.   Has a good job.

   _____ d.   Doesn't know the real value of money.

   _____ e.   Has a good head for business.

   _____ f.   Complains frequently about not having enough.

   _____ g.   Is a tightwad.

   _____ h.   Is career oriented.

   _____ i.   Always buys top-of-the-line merchandise.

   _____ j.   Likes garage sales.

2. Do you feel that your partner is more skilled than you at handling the family's finances? Why or why not?

   _____

   _____

   _____

   _____

   _____

   _____

   _____

   _____

   _____

3. What one item that your partner has given you do you treasure the most?

_____

_____

_____

_____

_____

_____

_____

_____

_____

4. Would you describe your partner as frugal or frivolous? Why?

_____

_____

_____

_____

_____

_____

_____

_____

_____

_____

▲▲▲▲▲▲▲▲▲▲▲▲▲▲▲▲▲▲▲▲▲▲▲▲▲▲▲▲▲▲▲▲▲▲▲▲▲

SECTION III

Coming Together

1. Now that you've heard of a budget, it's time to put one together.

    a. In the following blanks, list all of your assets and
        liabilities.This will give you an idea of your net worth.

ASSETS

	His	Hers	Combined
Savings			
Stocks			
Bonds			
Real Estate			
TOTALS			

▲▲▲▲▲▲▲▲▲▲▲▲▲▲▲▲▲▲▲▲▲▲▲▲▲▲▲▲▲▲▲▲▲

LIABILITIES (Total amounts owed)

	His	Hers	Combined
Credit Cards	_____	_____	_____
Real Estate	_____	_____	_____
Student Loans	_____	_____	_____
Car Loans	_____	_____	_____
Other loans	_____	_____	_____
_____	_____	_____	_____
_____	_____	_____	_____
_____	_____	_____	_____
_____	_____	_____	_____
_____	_____	_____	_____
_____	_____	_____	_____
_____	_____	_____	_____
TOTALS	_____	_____	_____

YOUR COMBINED NET WORTH

Total Combined Assets   _____

Minus

Total Combined Liabilities   _____

Equals

Combined Net Worth   _____

(Note: Assets should be more than liabilities, if not, you need to take action to improve your combined financial condition.)

▲▲▲▲▲▲▲▲▲▲▲▲▲▲▲▲▲▲▲▲▲▲▲▲▲▲▲▲▲▲▲▲▲▲▲▲▲▲

a.   In the following blank list all of your income and expenses. This will give you an idea of your discretionary income (money left over after paying all the bills).

INCOME

	His	Hers	Combined
Salary	_____	_____	_____
_____	_____	_____	_____
_____	_____	_____	_____
_____	_____	_____	_____
_____	_____	_____	_____
_____	_____	_____	_____
TOTALS	_____	_____	_____

YOUR COMBINED INCOME/EXPENSES

Total Combined Income   _____

Minus

Total Combined Monthly Expenses   _____

Equals

Combined Discretionary Income   _____

(Note: Income should be more than expenses, if not, you need to take action to improve your combined financial condition.)

MONTHLY EXPENSES (Monthly payment amounts)

	His	Hers	Combined
Mortgage/Rent	_____	_____	_____
Credit Card Payments	_____	_____	_____
	_____	_____	_____
	_____	_____	_____
Car Insurance	_____	_____	_____
Utilities	_____	_____	_____
Medical	_____	_____	_____
Car maintainance	_____	_____	_____
Home Repairs	_____	_____	_____
Food	_____	_____	_____
Clothing	_____	_____	_____
Various club dues	_____	_____	_____
Entertainment	_____	_____	_____
Savings/Investments	_____	_____	_____
Life Insurance	_____	_____	_____
School expenses	_____	_____	_____
_____	_____	_____	_____
_____	_____	_____	_____
_____	_____	_____	_____
_____	_____	_____	_____
_____	_____	_____	_____
_____	_____	_____	_____
_____	_____	_____	_____
TOTALS	_____	_____	_____

c.	Based on this exercise, figure your financial status. Are you overusing credit cards? Where can you find hidden monies in your expenses to reduce other debts?

_____

_____

_____

_____

_____

_____

_____

_____

d.	In your household, who is the spender and who is the saver? Discuss the advantages and disadvantages of separate and joint savings and checking accounts or a combination of separate and joint.

_____

_____

_____

_____

_____

_____

_____

_____

_____

_____

2. When you were growing up, did both your parents work, or was one of them home for most of the day? Was your father the main provider? What similarities or differences do you see in your expectations of your partner?

_____

_____

_____

_____

_____

_____

_____

_____

_____

_____

3. If your partner's career required that he or she relocate, how would you feel about giving up your career for your partner's advancement?

_____

_____

_____

_____

_____

_____

_____

_____

_____

4. If both partners work, how will home responsibilities be allotted? Make a list of chores and divide the list so that each person is comfortable with his or her assignment.

_____

_____

_____

_____

_____

_____

_____

_____

_____

_____

_____

_____

_____

_____

_____

_____

_____

_____

_____

_____

_____

_____

_____

_____

_____

CHAPTER SIX

FAMILY AND FRIENDS

Treat your friends like family and your family like friends. Family and friends are our own network. They support, encourage, meddle, criticize, care for, and love us. Our lives would be far less rich and meaningful without them.

Marriage has the potential to double our family and friends. With that single "I do" we suddenly inherit in-laws and our partner's friends as well. Our network multiplies and our relationships become more complex. Those family gatherings will never be the same. Dinner may consist of Uncle Arthur and his limericks and Aunt Mary Katherine's Bible verses, brother Pat's homosexuality, and Mom's pro-life preaching. And we all have a cousin Damien whom we try like mad to keep in the family closet.

Even with all the personality conflicts and differences in lifestyles, attitudes, and behavior, a new richness is added. Each person brings not only his quirks and hang-ups but also his insights, dreams, and perspectives. We might find Aunt Mary Katherine smiling at some of Uncle Arthur's limericks. And Uncle Arthur just might clean up his act a bit. And maybe our partner will even find something terrific about cousin Damien that everyone else overlooked.

Fitting everyone into the family picture takes some juggling and creativity. Do we spend Thanksgiving with her family or yours? In his home, gifts were opened on Christmas Eve, and in yours the big day was the twenty-fifth. He's used to his friends dropping by anytime, and we want to know exactly who's coming and when they're leaving. The ideal situation is for everyone to get along with everyone else, but of course this isn't always possible. It is important to recognize that relationships involve readjustment between our partner and our family and friends. Bringing together two new circles of people has its own particular stresses. Our hope is that our partner's life will mesh with ours and that we will live together harmoniously.

SECTION I

Personal Inventory

1. Fill in the blanks.

   a. I am the_____born in my family.

   b. I am accustomed to_____family gatherings.

   c. Every child is entitled to_____.

   d. My grandparents are_____.

   e. _____is my best friend.

   f. I get along_____with my siblings.

   g. Growing up, my family was ruled with_____
      and _____.

   h. I believe adoption is_____.

   i. I would like to have_____children.

   j. Holidays at our home were _____.

2. Based on the scale below, indicate the number that most closely represents your answer.

1—Strongly Agree
2—Mildly Agree
3—Not sure
4—Mildly Disagree
5—Strongly Disagree

_____ a.   Children should be seen and not heard.

_____ b.   Children learn more by example than by words.

_____ c.   Both partners should share parenting duties equally.

_____ d.   I get along very well with my partner's family.

_____ e.   My parents support my relationship with my partner.

_____ f.   Friends should feel free to drop by unannounced.

_____ g.   Family members should feel free to drop by unannounced.

_____ h.   It is okay for my partner to have friends of the opposite sex.

_____ i.   It is a bad practice to lend money to friends.

_____ j.   It is best to live a considerable distance from family and in-laws.

3. How and where would you like to spend your first Thanksgiving? Christmas?

_____

_____

_____

_____

_____

4. What customs or traditions in your home differ from those in your partner's?

_____

_____

_____

_____

_____

_____

_____

_____

_____

_____

_____

5. If you found out that your partner had been sexually, physically, or emotionally abused as a child, how would that affect your relationship?

_____

_____

_____

_____

_____

_____

_____

_____

SECTION II

Point of View

1. Answer the following either True or False.

    My partner...

    ____ a. Has a good relationship with his or her family.

    ____ b. Has strong family values.

    ____ c. Has friends of diverse cultural and ethnic backgrounds.

    ____ d. Trusts friends more than family.

    ____ e. Is comfortable around my family.

    ____ f. Enjoys spending time with my friends.

    ____ g. Shares my view on raising children.

    ____ h. Often asks his or her parents for advice.

    ____ i. Compares me to his or her mother or father.

2. Who are the mutual friends you and your partner share?

    _____

    _____

    _____

    _____

    _____

    _____

    _____

    _____

    _____

    _____

3. List the characteristics of your partner's best friend.

_____

_____

_____

_____

_____

_____

_____

4. Which member of your partner's family is he or she closest to? What makes that relationship special?

_____

_____

_____

_____

_____

_____

_____

5. If you could change one thing about the way your partner was raised, what would it be? Why?

_____

_____

_____

_____

_____

_____

_____

SECTION III

Coming Together

1. Create your own family album. Start by completing a family tree using the chart on the next page as a guideline. Your album could also include some or all of the following:

   ♦ noteworthy family history facts

   ♦ anecdotes and stories about growing up

   ♦ photos of family and favorite places

   ♦ your baby photos, copies of birth certificates, etc.

   ♦ news clippings of famous family members

   ♦ your first poem or love letter

   ♦ quotes from family, friends, and relatives

   ♦ stubs and brochures from your favorite outings

   ♦ passports

You can gather information and store it in a shoe box or plastic container until you agree on the type of album to use.

2. Discuss your family traditions. What are they? Which ones do you like? Dislike? What new traditions would you like to establish for your own family?

3. Establish guidelines for relating to in-laws. What expectations do your families have of you after marriage? How often will you communicate with them? How and where will you spend holidays?

4. Make a list of things you can do to let your parents and future in-laws know how important they are to you.

5. Discuss starting your own family. How soon after marriage would you like to have children? What basic principles do you have for parenting? How do you feel about adoption? If children or stepchildren are involved, how will you help them adjust to their new family?

Family Tree Outline

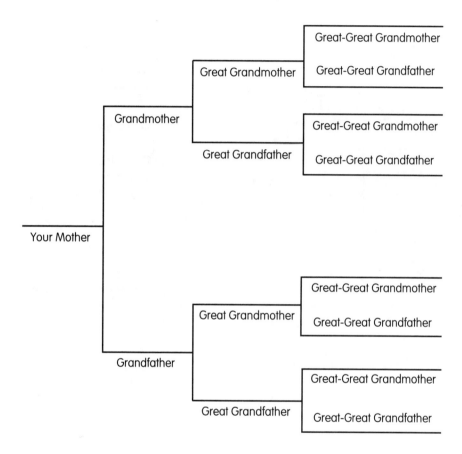

Note: Each of you should use separate sheets of paper to complete an outline for both of your parents.

Family Tree Outline

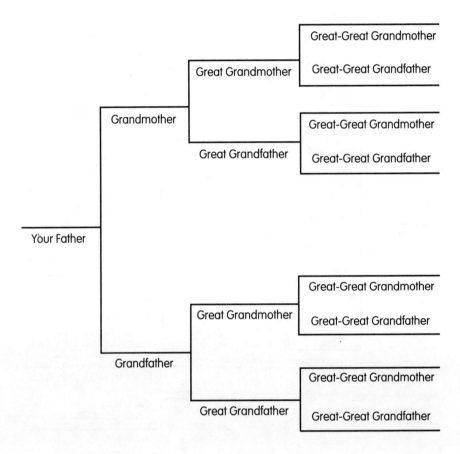

Note: Each of you should use separate sheets of paper to complete an outline for both of your parents.

CHAPTER SEVEN

COMMITMENT

Now we come to the very essence of marriage—commitment. Sound serious? It is.

What is commitment? Why do some of us fear it? Why do we put it off until later in life or avoid it altogether?

The society we live in now is one of choice and convenience. We have more choices than our parents ever dreamed possible. And talk about convenience. Everything we hear seems to tell us we can have everything we want whenever we want it.

If we don't like it, we dump it. The best of everything is our right, because we're worth it. No matter how great things are, someone comes along with a new, improved this or that. Sometimes we get caught up in the "have it my way" mentality. We find ourselves looking for the perfect job, car, house, book, hobby, partner.

Some of us approach marriage as a contract rather than as a commitment. Contracts contain conditional clauses, escape clauses that say "if"—if things don't go as expected, the deal's off. But marriage is a commitment, and commitment has no escape clause.*

Commitment takes work. It means rising above adversity. In the end, our relationship is whatever we make it. Each of us brings things to the relationship, and we build it from the ground up. A solid, sturdy foundation of commitment and strong morals and values must be laid first to provide stability and strength to weather the storms. We set our joists with respect, trust, and caring. We frame our walls with compromise and acceptance. We need plenty of windows for communication. Finally, we put on the roof of love to cover, protect, and nurture.

Marriage can be one of the most fulfilling unions between two people. But good marriages don't just happen; they are created by the people in them.

*If you are in an abusive relationship, however, seek help immediately.

Goals and Purpose

Goals are measurable. If you say you want to lose weight, you are stating a purpose. If you say you want to lose ten pounds by June, then you are stating a goal.

Goals are

- •stated in terms of the end result
- •achievable within a definite time period
- •specific about what is expected
- •practical and feasible
- •stated in one important statement.

SECTION I

Personal Inventory

1.   Complete the following statements.

Trust means

_____

_____

Divorce means

_____

_____

Marriage means

_____

_____

Faithfulness in marriage means

_____

_____

Commitment means

_____

_____

2. What goals do you have for your marriage?

3. What are some fears and anxieties you have about marriage?

_____

_____

_____

_____

_____

_____

_____

_____

_____

_____

_____

_____

_____

_____

_____

_____

_____

_____

_____

_____

4. What commitments, if any, have you made in your life? (Include those you have made to a person, cause, ideology, religion, or sport.) How did you fulfill those commitments?

5. What do the words "For better or worse, for richer or poorer, in sickness and in health" mean to you?

_____

_____

_____

_____

_____

_____

_____

_____

_____

_____

_____

_____

_____

_____

_____

_____

_____

_____

_____

_____

_____

_____

SECTION II

Point of View

1. Answer the following either True or False.

   My partner...

   _____ a. Understands and fulfills my emotional needs.

   _____ b. Sticks to commitments no matter what.

   _____ c. Expects me to read his or her mind.

   _____ d. Respects my opinions even if they differ from his or hers.

   _____ e. Makes assumptions about how I will respond to situations.

   _____ f. Believes our relationship will never change.

   _____ g. Is very demanding.

   _____ h. Shares my goals for our marriage.

   _____ i. Handles adversity well.

   _____ j. Is realistic about life.

2. How does your partner handle responsibility?

   _____

   _____

   _____

   _____

   _____

   _____

   _____

   _____

3. When was the last time you and your partner had a disagreement? What were the circumstances? How did you make up?

_____

_____

_____

_____

_____

_____

_____

_____

_____

4. How has your partner changed from when you first met? Are these changes for the better or for worse?

_____

_____

_____

_____

_____

_____

_____

_____

_____

_____

_____

▲▲▲▲▲▲▲▲▲▲▲▲▲▲▲▲▲▲▲▲▲▲▲▲▲▲▲▲▲▲▲

SECTION III

Coming Together

Most of us, if not all, enter a relationship with our own agenda. We don't bother to clue our partner in, because we just assume our partner will somehow know what we want and expect. We think: This is the way my parents did it, so every other family must do it this way too. We don't stop to think that our way isn't the only way. But when our partner fails to fit into our mold, perform certain tasks the way mom and dad did it, or respond emotionally to our unvoiced needs we feel frustrated, hurt, angry.

We hit our first brick wall when we realize our partner's expectations differ from ours. Some expectations are quite legitimate, others are unrealistic and simply can not be fulfilled by our partner. We must evaluate our expectations in order to weed out the legitimate from the unrealistic.

> 1. List ten expectations you have of your partner. Think about how your life and marriage will be affected if that expectation is never met. Share the list with your partner so that he or she can look at and evaluate each expectation. You can respond to each expectation with one of the following statements.

I can meet this expectation:

> a.   most of the time
>
> b.   some of the time

OR

It would be difficult for me to meet this expectation because . . .

Ask your partner why eacy expectation is important to him/her. If you can not meet the expectation ask your partner how he or she will be affected and if the expectation can be adjusted.

Ten Expectations

1. _____

_____

2. _____

_____

3. _____

_____

4. _____

_____

5. _____

_____

6. _____

_____

7. _____

_____

8. _____

_____

9. _____

_____

10. _____

_____

2. Describe the decision-making process that you think you will have in your marriage. Indicate the percentage of influence you will have for each issue. The total of each decision must be 100%.

	Hers	His	Who is best qualified to make this decision
Wife's career	_____	_____	_____
Husband's career	_____	_____	_____
Household Budget	_____	_____	_____
Major purchases	_____	_____	_____
Household tasks	_____	_____	_____
Birth control	_____	_____	_____
When and how often to have sex	_____	_____	_____
How and when to entertain friends	_____	_____	_____
How and when to entertain members of wife's family	_____	_____	_____

How and when to entertain
members of husband's _____   _____   _____
family

Vacations _____   _____   _____

How many children to have _____   _____   _____

Where family lives _____   _____   _____

Family activities _____   _____   _____

_____   _____   _____   _____

_____   _____   _____   _____

_____   _____   _____   _____

_____   _____   _____   _____

_____   _____   _____   _____

3.   Write out a commitment statement to your partner.

_____

_____

_____

_____

_____

_____

_____

_____

_____

_____

_____

_____

_____

HOTLINES

NATIONAL INSTITUTE ON DRUG ABUSE

1-800-662-4357

Provides alcohol and other drug treatment referrals. Has information on self-help groups, various hotlines, and treatment programs.

CALIFORNIA SELF-HELP CENTER

1-800-222-5465 (California only)

10 am-4 pm Mon-Fri

Statewide consumer resource for finding, forming, and maintaining self-help and mutual support groups.

NATIONAL COALITION AGAINST DOMESTIC VIOLENCE

1-303-839-1852

NATIONAL CHILD ABUSE HOTLINE

1-800-422-4453

AIDS HOTLINE

1-800-342-2437 TDD 1-800-243-7889

Provides referrals and information regarding legal services, education, information dissemination, research, financial aid, counseling, medical treatment and services, support groups, referrals to testing sites.

SUGGESTED READING LIST

1. His Needs, Her Needs: Building An Affair-Proof Marriage. Willard F. Harley, Jr. City, State: Fleming H. Revell Company, 1986.

2. You Just Don't Understand: Women and Men in Conversation. Deborah Tannen. City, State: William Morrow and Company, Inc. 1990.

3. Marital Myths. Arnold A. Lazarus. City, State: Impact Publishers, 1985.

4. Secrets About Men Every Woman Should Know. Barbara De Angelis. City, State: Dell, 1990.

BIBLIOGRAPHY

Lederer, William J. <u>Marital Choices</u>. New York: W.W. Norton & Company, Inc., 1981.

Poteet, David. <u>How to Trace Your Family Tree</u>. City, Minn.: Jeremy Books, 1977.

Sedgwick, Sherry. <u>The Good Sex Book: Recovering and Discovering Your Sexual Self</u>. City, Minn.: CompCare Publishers, 1992.

Wright, Norman H. <u>So You're Getting Married.</u> City, Calif.: Regal Books, 1985.

ABOUT THE AUTHOR

Betsy Summers has spent a lifetime observing and enduring turbulent relationships. When she was three, her parents divorced and proceeded to marry and divorce other partners regularly until Betsy was eighteen. Along the way, she accumulated a sister, four half-brothers, and various other stepsiblings.

In 1985, determined not to repeat the matrimonial mayhem of her parents, Betsy married her high school sweetheart. Although the couple had been best friends for fourteen years, they were strangers to the complexities of a successful marriage. Her intended had one divorce behind him and then broke his engagement to another woman to marry Betsy.

As wedded bliss gave way to marital misery, Betsy realized that healthy marriage relationships need stronger foundations than friendship, familiarity, or physical attraction. She started doing research for Look Before You Leap in 1986. Her marriage ended in divorce in 1989.

Today, Betsy and her six-year-old son, Mason, live in Los Angeles.

NOTES